Macaroni
and Rice
and Bread
by the Slice

to Mrs. Somlai, my fourth-grade teacher in Richfield, Minnesota, and to
Mrs. Simoneau, my (second) fourth-grade teacher in Rocky River, Ohio
—B.P.C.

to my wife, Geneviève, the kernel of my life
—M.G.

Grain:
The seeds
from a grass
crop grown
for food

Macaroni and Rice and Bread by the Slice

What Is in the Grains Group?

by Brian P. Cleary

illustrations by Martin Goneau

consultant Jennifer K. Nelson, Master of Science,
Registered Dietitian, Licensed Dietitian

M Millbrook Press · Minneapolis

Grains are the seeds from a cereal plant.

Some are as small as a new baby ant!

But when you learn more
and you get the whole scoop,

you'll find they're a HUGE
and important food group.

This edible crop
may be starchy or grassy.

A grain can be wholesome
or twisted
or classy.

6

How much should you eat?

Well, in case you are tested:
five to six ounces
each day is suggested.

The two types of grains
are called whole and refined.
Let's look at them both,
so you'll know either kind.

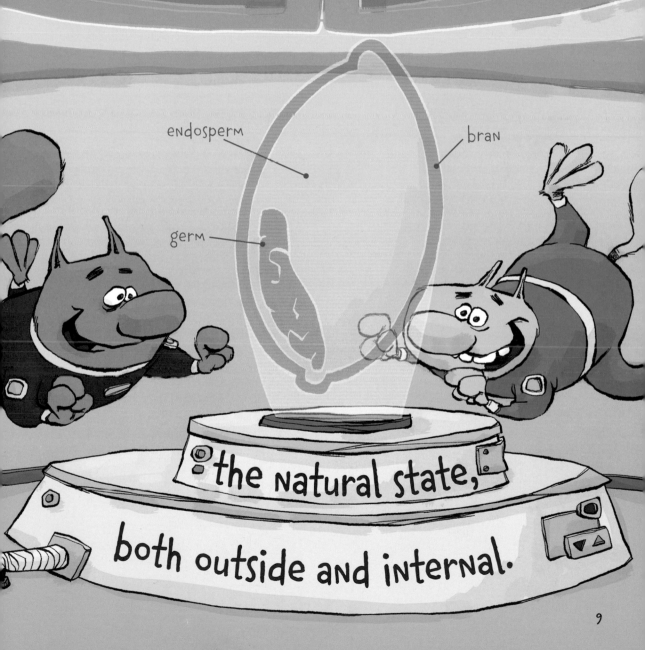

Whole grains include
all the parts of the kernel—

the natural state,
both outside and internal.

9

Popcorn is whole grain.

And so's wild rice,

oatmeal, and buckwheat,

so heed this advice:

whether in whole wheat pastas or rolls,

in the course of each day,
half your grains
should be whole.

Whole grains are found
in some cereals too.

Muesli, bran,
and Whole Wheat are a few.

They're loaded with fiber—
a friend to your body.
They help you digest food
and make you go potty.

Foods high in fiber
are also quite good
    at helping your heart
    to do all that it should.

Eating whole grains
each and every day thrice

may help fight heart problems.

So pass the brown rice!

The other grain type
is what's known as refined.

That white bread and white rice
on which you have dined?

They're part of that group,
like enriched rigatoni,
grits,
crackers,
corn bread,
and most macaroni.

Sometimes, the evening before a big meet,

a long-distance runner will sit down to eat.

In his or her bowl,
pasta's filled to the brim.

This helps boost endurance
for her or for him.

For you to be
truly an expert on grain,

there are cereal facts
that you'll need to retain.

Some grains come from oats—
Some from wheat, rice, or corn.

Sometimes they're flaked,
others, puffy when formed.

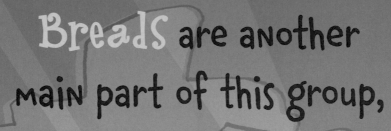

Breads are another
main part of this group,

whether used for your sandwich
or dipped in your soup.

22

And how about crackers?

They come from a grain
that grows from the soil
and is fed by the rain.

That grain grows in sunlight
in rows on a field.

And ends up in crackers
all boxed up and sealed.

You may find your grains
in a food that is crispy,

curly, or crunchy,

so light that it's wispy.

It might be all flaky
or puffy or sweet.

Or ready to POP when it's placed over heat.

So now you're a scholar,
an expert on grain—
with facts stored like wheat
in your silo-type brain.

When folks seek your wisdom,
they'll see much more there

than a small grain of truth
in each fact that you share.

So what is in the grains group? Do you know?

You should eat 5 to 6 ounces of grains every day. The exact amount depends on your age and how much exercise you get. To figure out the right amount for you, visit www.MyPyramid.gov and click on MyPyramid Plan.

  1 slice whole wheat bread equals 1 ounce

3 cups popcorn equals 1 ounce

 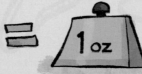 5 whole wheat crackers equals 1 ounce

1/2 cup oatmeal equals 1 ounce

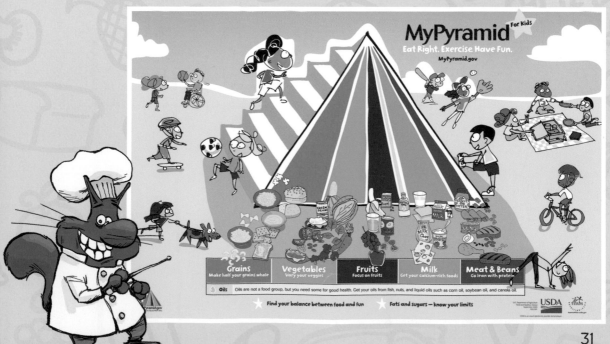

31

This book provides general
dietary information for children
ages 5–9 in accordance with the
MyPyramid guidelines created by the
United States Department of Agriculture (USDA).
The information in this book is not intended as medical advice. Anyone with food allergies
or sensitivities should follow the advice of a physician or other medical professional.

Find activities, games, and more at
www.brianpcleary.com

ABOUT THE AUTHOR, ILLUSTRATOR & CONSULTANT

BRIAN P. CLEARY is the author of the Words Are Categorical®, Math Is Categorical®,
Adventures in Memory™, Sounds Like Reading®, and Food Is CATegorical™ series,
as well as several picture books and poetry books. He lives in Cleveland, Ohio.

MARTIN GONEAU is the illustrator of the Food Is CATegorical™ series. He lives in
Trois-Rivières, Québec.

JENNIFER K. NELSON is Director of Clinical Dietetics and Associate Professor in
Nutrition at Mayo Clinic in Rochester, Minnesota. She is also a Specialty Medical
Editor for nutrition and healthy eating content for MayoClinic.com.

Millbrook Press
A division of Lerner Publishing Group, Inc.
241 First Avenue North
Minneapolis, MN 55401 U.S.A.

Website address: www.lernerbooks.com

Library of Congress Cataloging-in-Publication Data

Cleary, Brian P., 1959–
    Macaroni and rice and bread by the slice : what is in the grains group? / by Brian P. Cleary ; illustrated by Martin Goneau ;
consultant Jennifer K. Nelson.
        p.   cm. — (Food Is CATegorical)
    ISBN: 978–1–58013–587–0 (lib. bdg. : alk. paper)
    1. Cereals as food—Juvenile literature. 2. Grain in human nutrition—Juvenile literature. I. Goneau, Martin. II. Nelson,
Jennifer K. III. Title.
    TX393.C54 2011
    641.3'31—dc22   2009049194

Manufactured in the United States of America
1 – PC – 7/15/10